"The Bishop Must Be…"

Dr. Gregory Pittman Sr.

© Copyright 2025

Dr. Gregory Pittman Sr.

Printed in the United States of America

All rights reserved. No part of this book can be reproduced in any form without the express written permission from the author, except in the case of brief quotations, critical articles or reviews.

GPS PUBLISHING L.L.C.

1315Oakfield Dr. Ste. 2914

Brandon, FL 33509

gpspublishing2662@gmail.com

All scripture unless otherwise noted are from the King James Version of the Bible.

ISBN 979-8-9899177-3-0

Other books by Dr. Gregory Pittman Sr. available on Amazon.com

Dedication

To God be the glory for all the things He has done in my life and with my life. Only the mistakes are mine any accomplishments are due to Him and the great men and woman he has allowed to pour substance into my walk with Jesus Christ. Besides my mother, the late Evangelist Dr. Fannie A. Pittman, my greatest mentor and spiritual father was the Late Bishop James F. Copeland. He was an amazing man of God who taught me how to walk by faith and to hold onto God's unchanging had. He saw something in me that God wanted to bring out of me and encouraged me to pursue what Christ was calling me to be. I wish he were here today to see what he saw in me. Here was a true Bishop and father indeed. Not just to me but many, many others were drawn by his shepherding, and genuine love for people.

To the man of God who was the first man ever to call me "son," I dedicate this work to you who was and still is the standard of the bishopric. I still remember your words when you would say: "**Only what you do for God will Last!**"

Thank you, Lord for Bishop James F. Copeland!!!!!!!!

Back cover photo: Dr. Gregory Pittman Sr. & The Late Bishop James F. Copeland

TABLE OF CONTENTS

Dedication…………………….....iv

Introduction……………………….8

1. The Bishop…………………...15
2. Blameless……………….…32
3. Husband………………….....46
4. Vigilant………………………60
5. Sober…………………………66
6. Of Good behavior……………73
7. Not a Brawler………………..95
8. Not Covetous……………….100
9. One that rules his house well.107
10. Not a Novice………………...112
11. Must have a good report…….116
12. The Bishop Today………...…120

"THE BISHOP MUST BE…"

INTRODUCTION

A Bishop must be, is not an implication but is a definitive statement of a fact. It states that there is a qualification built upon principles, not rules which are subjective, but firmly established upon principles which are not swayed by outside influences, but are completely objective and stand alone as the only qualifier, for anyone who desires to ascend into the office of a bishop. First, there is a proposition that a candidate for the office must first have an earnest desire to do the work of a bishop. "This is a true saying, if a man desires the office of a bishop, he desires a good work." This therefore must be the first qualification to be fulfilled, for the office

"THE BISHOP MUST BE…"

of a "bishop." Without a passion for the work, the work cannot be passionately done. If your heart isn't in it why sit in the seat?

Now we come to the question of what, and why, of qualifications. There are prerequisites in every aspect of our lives, and Christian Ministry is no different, as a matter of fact the Christian walk should supersede all other qualifiers because it directly affects the way in which the entire community of men can and cannot view God Almighty. The standards of Christ are raised by the sanctified believer not by carnal impulses. Qualifications are therefore an essential foundation upon which the ministry of a

"THE BISHOP MUST BE…"

bishop is authenticated. Some have interpreted this to include all ministry positions which is admirable because we should always seek the highest standards in all that we aspire to do, excellence is the Christian way or should be (Col 1:10).

First things first, instead of answering the why, or the, what is, we should first establish the ultimate qualifier, the definitive qualifier is: "sola scriptura" a Latin term meaning scripture alone. There is nothing that authenticates the Christian life, walk and practice than the infallible, inerrant, written word of God. There is no greater testimony than the witness of Jesus Christ, He is the

"THE BISHOP MUST BE…"

WORD made flesh. Scripture alone qualifies or disqualifies us for the work and service within the Kingdom of God, our eternal destiny is determined by how we respond to the word of God (John 3:16, 18).

The American Heritage Dictionary defines qualification as a quality or an ability that makes a person suitable for a particular position or task. Quality is a degree of excellence, distinctive attributes, character, or traits that qualify you or make you competent for an office, position, or task. Therefore, the office of a Bishop is an office that an individual must qualify for, not just assume or usurp, but certain standards must be met and maintained along with the initial

"THE BISHOP MUST BE…"

desire for the work of the bishop. Just as there are certain essentials that would qualify someone for the office, there are also disqualifiers that would prevent someone from the office and also to disqualify some who are already in the office. We should never assume that just because someone met the qualifications for the office at a particular time, and later on violated one or several of the principles of that office, that they are to function in that office without any accountability this is unscriptural, and has its basis in the doctrine of devils. Nowhere in scripture do we find anyone in authority, who was not subjected to a principle of accountability. Moses was forbidden to enter

"THE BISHOP MUST BE…"

the promise land because in one moment of anger he disobeyed God. King David, could not build the Temple of God because he had broken the commandment "thou shalt not kill (Exodus 20:13)."

God exiled both the northern and southern kingdoms of Israel and Judah because they disqualified themselves as a covenant keeping nation by transgressing the Law of the Lord. There are many instances where someone was put into an office and by their actions or negligence were rejected from that office (1Sam. 15:20-28).

God has an order and everything must be done according to His standard of excellence without compromise, He gave Moses specific

"THE BISHOP MUST BE…"

instructions on the qualifications for the office of the priesthood, and disqualified any that had blemishes from serving in the priestly functions. The Apostle Paul received specific instruction regarding the ministry of the bishop, the eldership, the deaconate and the order of the church itself. Nothing is left to the carnal mind of men, but all things are done according to the spirit of Christ and that which He has revealed through His Holy Word.

"THE BISHOP MUST BE…"

1

THE BISHOP

"This is a true saying, if a man desires the office of a bishop; he desires a good work (1Timothy 3:1)."

Sola Scriptura – from the very first day I heard and understood this term I embraced it as much as I had embraced it before I ever heard of this Latin term – meaning scripture alone.

My intention from the time of my conversion, from a sinner to a believer in Christ has been to do the will of God, not just to the best of my ability but to the glory of God. My

"THE BISHOP MUST BE…"

mentors throughout my Christian walk since it began in 1985 have continually stressed the significance of the word of God as not just the final authority but, the only authority that is inerrant and infallible. I have been in total agreement with this assessment, not because of their word, but because of God's word and the witness of the Holy Spirit. I believe God's word is truth because He has demonstrated to me that He never fails to honor that which He has spoken. His word is truth, and His truth is the truth. He is eternally faithful to His truth, because it is saturated with His Holiness and His righteous character. His word displays His integrity and forbids Him to act against Himself. His

"THE BISHOP MUST BE..."

word is the standard by which all things are measured.

I believe God gives us assignments to fulfill His purpose and plans, at times we may not understand why He chose us, but He knows the reason. I can think of so many people, who are more qualified to do this assignment besides myself, and I have made it known to God, but He continued to burden me with this subject. Why? Because of the abuses witnessed daily throughout the institution known as the Church of God. The answer to this question is yes and no. I believe it is because He created me with a desire to see

"THE BISHOP MUST BE…"

His Word, His Truth, His Righteousness, His Love, and His Holiness becomes the way, the truth and the life on earth, especially through the Church. I believe God knows that His Church is out of sync, and has conformed to the ways of society, instead of society conforming to the revealed will of God through the agency of His Church. I believe that God is seeking to restore order to His Church and He will begin with the leaders of the Church. This is nothing new in how the Lord deals with His people; He always starts from the top down. The Lord has imparted within me a love for Him and His word, and a love for the Church of Jesus Christ. God knows that giving me this assignment would

"THE BISHOP MUST BE…"

not be done from a posture of malice, but for the love of God and the perfecting of the Church of the Living God.

This statement is worthy of acceptance, that if a man "desires" the position of a bishop he desires a work that is good! With this desire we must understand that there are always qualifications, when one is in pursuit of this office or any office of leadership. In school we were taught that if someone wanted to become president of the United States of America, a certain criterion had to be met first before he or she could consider running

"THE BISHOP MUST BE…"

for the office of president. These prerequisites were simply, any candidate must be a natural born citizen of the United States of America, and they must be at least thirty-five years of age or older. As we were taught these were the only qualifications any candidate needed to campaign for the office of the presidency of the United States of America. Nothing more was necessary for candidacy.

A candidate for the office of a bishop requires prerequisites also, but it requires one to be much more than a born-again believer, and a walk that is far removed from that of a novice. Although, they are essential

"THE BISHOP MUST BE…"

qualities, this high office requires more than citizenship and age. This is a superior office than the presidency of the United States, or any other earthly office of any nation, and therefore demands a greater standard. Because it is a spiritual office and not a natural one it necessitates not only natural qualities, but, spiritual endowments that must be evident.

When looking at the term "bishop" we must understand that the word generally means "overseer." The word "bishop" is derived from the Greek word episcope (pronounced ep-is-kop-ay), which by implication means

"THE BISHOP MUST BE…"

superintendence, which means to be responsible for the management or arrangement of an activity or organization; it is overseeing as in the case of the ecclesia a living organism. This particular word appears five times in the New Testament, twice in reference to visitation (Lu. 19:44; 1 Pet. 2:12), once in (1Tim. 3:1), one time as bishopric (Acts 1:20) and in reference to the office in (1Tim. 3:1). This office or position of a bishop was not, nor was it ever intended to be an office where the office holder had absolute authority and no accountability to anyone. The Greek word designates pastoral oversight, over a local area or congregation. A bishop or the word "bishop" expresses the

"THE BISHOP MUST BE…"

meaning of supervisor or one who oversees. Paul in his letter to Titus uses the words "elder" or "presbyter" to refer to the same office as the "bishop" (Titus 1:5-9).

Ambition is not it enough for the position. We know politicians have an ambitious nature and a strong desire for the power that a particular office may hold. And they are typically, not concerned with the responsibility for which they must be accountable to. They always talk about being for the people but seldom politic the will of the people. Usually, their politicking is based upon a particular party line and rarely will they vote contrary to their party affiliation,

"THE BISHOP MUST BE..."

for they know that their re-election depends upon party support.

God always required His leaders to adhere to the strict set of principles, because His leaders represented Him, and His Righteous Kingdom, and they must always be of the highest attribute. He would have loved to have perfect beings, but that wasn't one of the requirements that was required, if so, Jesus Christ would be the only one qualified because He alone was sinless.

When speaking to Moses regarding the Aaronic Priesthood, He gave specific instructions for the office of the priest, and also the office of high priest. The first qualification was, they had to be a descendant

"THE BISHOP MUST BE…"

from Aaron, which meant although someone was from the Levitical priestly tribe, that did not qualify one for priestly duties or office. Those that met the qualifications as a descendant of Aaron, must go through further screening. For instance, God commanded Aaron in Leviticus 10:9, that priests are not allowed to drink wine or intoxicating drink while performing ministry in the tabernacle, knowing that this would impair their ability to make wise conclusions or resolutions. And this requirement was to assure "that they may distinguish between holy and unholy, and between clean and unclean, and that you may teach the children of Israel all the statues

"THE BISHOP MUST BE…"

which the Lord has spoken to them by the hand of Moses (Lev. 10:10,11)."

Furthermore, there were more restrictions pertaining to the office of the priest and the high priest. In Leviticus 21, the Lord told Moses to "speak to the priests" and remind them of the purity and holiness of their exclusive office as sons of Aaron, and to be careful to preserve themselves because they presented the sacred offerings unto God on behalf of a holy nation. In verse one He instructs them never to defile themselves "for the dead among his people" except for close relatives (Lev. 21:1). In Leviticus chapter 21:10-12, forbids the high priest from mourning or even attending funeral services

"THE BISHOP MUST BE..."

for any family including his parents while he was high priest serving before the LORD (Lev. 21:11). Further stipulations for the office of priest and high priest involved marriage. For instance, a priest was forbidden to "…take a wife that is a harlot, or is defiled; neither shall they take a woman put away from her husband: for he is holy unto his God" (Lev. 21:7). The requirements for the priesthood were stringent, even upon their personal life, because their personal life influenced their professional life, and their professional service to the Lord should also have a great influence upon their personal life. A high priest was restricted even more when it came to marriage, if anyone desired

"THE BISHOP MUST BE…"

to become high priest he had to take a wife in her virginity, "And he that is the high priest among his brethren, upon whose head the anointing oil was poured, and that is consecrated to put on the garments… he shall take a wife in her virginity. (Lev. 21:10, 13)." If he did not then he would automatically be disqualified for the office of high priest. He was also required to have his house in order for, Leviticus 21:9 tells us that "…the daughter of any priest, if she defiles herself by playing the harlot, she defiles her father: she shall be burned with fire." Other exclusions from the priesthood were physical defects, i.e. a man blind or lame, marred face or a limb to long (Lev. 21:16-24). Simply

"THE BISHOP MUST BE…"

put the potential priest or high priest had to meet clear-cut specifications that qualified a descendant of Aaron to become a priest, there were also things that disqualified him from the priesthood. It was nothing personal against anyone, it's just the Lord had a particular standard for them that served in His name and served His people.

The Lord yet has high standards to which He holds everyone who has a desire to minister in His name. These qualifiers that the apostle Paul sets forth in 1 Timothy 3, for church leaders, including deacons is so that the church of the living God would be the pattern that would be emulated. Therefore, the meticulous qualifications must begin with

"THE BISHOP MUST BE..."

leadership. Now we understand that the word "bishop" in verse 1 means "overseer and by extension refers to "elders," but, this is a set of standards that God desires all of His people to aspire unto. A descendant of Aaron did not know if he would become high priest or not, but, if he desired the position, it would behoove him if he made sure he followed the qualifiers for the office of high priest. Even so, each believer should always strive towards the mark of the high calling in Christ Jesus. We could be propelled into ministry, so each of us should live as if we are the leadership of the Most High God. These qualifications to become a bishop are definitely meant for any leadership position

"THE BISHOP MUST BE…"

in the church. No one should ever be appointed unless he or she can meet the highest standards for Christian leadership regardless of their talent.

"THE BISHOP MUST BE…"

2

BLAMELESS

"A bishop must be…blameless," we come to the first and probably most important aspect of the life pertaining to "a bishop." First apostle Paul commended the desire one might have for the work of a bishop; I say work rather than office because it is more than having a title, this position required a substantial amount of time and effort and was not to be taken likely, and today the standard is the same. Whosoever desires the office of a bishop desires a good work, meaning toil or labor, not just a seat, a robe, a ring and a

"THE BISHOP MUST BE…"

chain, and the best seating at ecclesiastical functions. The bishop was put through a vetting process, which needs to be

reinstituted and strictly enforced today. After the desire for the office then came the process for verifying if the candidate was worthy to be installed into the bishopric.

Blameless, means innocent of wrongdoing, it also means virtuous, faultless, spotless and irreproachable. Is there a person who fits into this definition? This word "blameless" differs from Luke 1:6; and Philippians 2:15; 3:6, in that it is referring to a life lived without fault, and here in 1 Timothy 3:2 the notion exceeds the life lived, but it transcends towards outward testimonies regarding the

"THE BISHOP MUST BE…"

Christian walk observed by others. Being blameless or having a blameless life is one that garners a testimony to the fact that the love of God is evident in your everyday walk. It shines as a glowing testimony that Jesus is the Christ the Son of the Living God, and that He is alive and is standing before you right now, through me. Being blameless, is being Christ like, it is being inculpable, meaning that you are not only without fault and without blame, but you cannot be accused by anyone, believer or non-believer. Being blameless is being beyond reproach. This suggests that a bishop's life is an impeachable life, it's a life that every

"THE BISHOP MUST BE…"

Christian is supposed to, not only aspire to but live, consistently and relentlessly. This is where Paul establishes a principle of truth. What is the principle of truth? The principle is a bishop must be blameless. Here the door is opened and a foundation is laid that is intricately woven into every other requirement for this great and noble office. Being blameless is the essential attribute present because it is not only upholding the rest that follows but must be interwoven into every aspect of the life of every believer, especially a potential candidate for the bishop's office. It is as essential to a Christian leader as God's Holiness is to His character and His attributes. How essential is

"THE BISHOP MUST BE…"

it? God's Holiness is so indispensable that if it were possible to detached God's Holiness form Him, every other attribute, such as His Righteousness, Faithfulness, Mercy, Lovingkindness, Longsuffering, etc., would cease to be what they are. His Righteousness therefore, would not be perfect, and would fail to be the ultimate perfection of Righteousness. Consequently, if the character of a bishop could be impeached his appointment to the office would have to be negated. This is the core of what it means to be a bishop, he must be scrupulous. This is a necessary composition for an aspirant for the office.

"THE BISHOP MUST BE…"

1 Timothy 3:2 is not suggesting that as a necessary precondition for office a bishop should be perfect, but that he should be a man against whom no charge of immorality or the embracing of false doctrine can be alleged. The life of the candidate must be free from scandal, and be an exemplary life that shines so bright, that others may not only behold it but, admire it, and want to emulate it. To be blameless also means one is vigilant, taking care to always portray the living Christ in a glorious light.

Adam Clarke in his commentary writes: a Christian bishop must be blameless; a person against whom no evil can be proved; one who is everywhere invulnerable; for the word is a

"THE BISHOP MUST BE…"

metaphor, taken from the case of an expert and skillful pugilist, who so defends every part of his body that it is impossible for his antagonist to give one hit. So, this Christian bishop is one that has so conducted himself, as to put it out of the reach of any person to prove that he is either unsound in a single article of the Christian faith, or deficient in the fulfillment of any duty incumbent on a Christian. He must be irreprehensible; for how can he reprove that in others which they can reprove in him?

Today more than ever there is an urgent need for men and women of God to not only mimic a blameless lifestyle but to actually be blameless in character and in deeds. This

"THE BISHOP MUST BE…"

sought of believer will turn the world upside down, and even the accuser of the brethren will have no defense because there will be no area in which he might have an occasion to indict the man or woman of God.

Blameless does not mean perfect, because only God is perfect, and we are pressing our way towards He who is perfect. God tells us to be holy as He is holy, expressing the idea that we can be holy as the Lord is holy. God would not command us to do something that would be impossible to do. Instead, He supplies all the resources we need to fulfill His every command. Being blameless doesn't mean we become mistake free, it simply means that we live in a committed life

"THE BISHOP MUST BE…"

patterned after our savior. Moses a great man of God was forbidden to enter into the Promised Land because he acted outside the will of God for a brief moment. But later testimonies say; "And Moses verily was faithful in all his house, as a servant, for a testimony of those things which were to be spoken later (Hebrews 3:5)."

The Apostle Peter wrote in his second epistle says; "beloved, I now write unto you; in both of which I stir up your pure minds…" Here the Greek word for "pure" is eilikrines (pronounced eye-lik-ree-nace), and is literally translated "tested by sun light." This conveys the thought of judging something by sunlight to uncover any flaws. Peter wanted

"THE BISHOP MUST BE…"

to stir up the pureness of the Christian mindset free of falsehood and foreign hidden motives. In the fourteenth verse of chapter three Peter again addresses the blameless life of all believers. His words were; "be diligent," and "to be found by Him in peace, without spot and blameless." Paul confirms Peter's affirmation speaking to the Corinthian Church he states, that God "will also confirm you to the end…blameless…" This suggests that not just a bishop but all believers must present themselves holy and blameless, above reproach in the sight of God. God has a desire to have a glorious Church without spot, wrinkle or blemish. Rooted and built up in Him, this must, most assuredly be the

"THE BISHOP MUST BE…"

posture of a bishop, without spot and blameless. David the Psalmist as expressed in the 19th Psalm verse 12 asks "who can understand?" Understand what? What does he want us to discern, perceive, grasp, consider and regard? What should we have insight into? Was he referring to errors? No, he was talking about cleansing. Recall the preceding verses, he was proclaiming that God's law, His statues, His precepts were not only perfect but has a converting power unequaled, which causes one to be wise, joyous and enlightening, and possessing them are of the greatest value which brings forth great rewards. So now he says who can understand errors? An error means a state or

"THE BISHOP MUST BE…"

condition of being wrong in conduct or judgment, which every believer can and must be free from. We just need to embrace the Word of God fully without equivocation.

Next, he draws our attention to the positive by declaring "cleanse me from secret…" The word fault does not appear in the original texts. He was praying a prophetic prayer, for himself and for all believers. It was prophetic because, it was the revealed will of God, for all believers, to be blameless and the presumptuous sins would never dominate the believer's life. David employs a Hebrew word "Nagah (pronounced Nah-kah)" which occurs some 39 times in the Old Testament, it literally means to clear, acquit, cleanse, to

"THE BISHOP MUST BE…"

make clean as we are cleansed by the efficacious blood of Jesus Christ. It also carries the meaning of making blameless, free or to exempt. It also suggests that one becomes blameless, not on his or her volition but, because of the Divine act of emptying, as if pouring out the contents that are contrary to the Lord God. As one would empty out a cup of its contents and replace them with something much more desirable, precious and better. Lord, cleanse me from secret faults, and the bishop must be blameless without ambiguousness. He must seek daily to extricate and extirpate anything in his life that would seek to uproot, destroy, and exterminate the plan and purpose of God, for

"THE BISHOP MUST BE…"

his life and the life of the Church. He must take care to entangle himself in anything that

would bring a reproach upon God, the Church, the office of the bishop and every believer must be blameless!

"THE BISHOP MUST BE…"

3

Husband

A bishop must be…"the husband of one wife." Out of all the prescribed requirements for this great office, I think here is where we see the greatest controversy. This qualification seems to stimulate the most debate. There are countless views upon what this could actually mean, does it mean has to be married? Or does it mean he cannot remarry after a divorce? Could it possibly mean that divorce excludes him from the office of the bishop? Or, if he was married and divorced before salvation, and remarried in the Lord would this be an impediment to

"THE BISHOP MUST BE…"

serving in the office of a bishop? This and many more questions arise when this subject is broached in Christendom.

I believe the answer lies in the will of God, and knowing the will of God concerning marriage and exercising it instead of our will, would clear up any misunderstanding. But what is the holy intention of the Lord God regarding marriage, especially for the bishop?

The first thing we can conclude from Paul's letter to Timothy is that he does not invoke apostolic authority, and proclaims that office pursuers must be celibate. No, he emphatically by this statement "husband of one wife" sanction marriage of bishops. So,

"THE BISHOP MUST BE…"

to them that teach and believe that the clergy must be unmarried, and declaring it as a doctrine of the church, you are walking in and teaching error. Paul addressed this particular subject to Timothy in the fourth chapter when talking about the great apostasy, he said:

1 Timothy 4:1-3 "Now the Spirit speaketh expressly, that in the latter times some shall depart from the faith, giving heed to seducing spirits, and doctrines of devils; Speaking lies in hypocrisy; having their conscience seared with a hot iron; Forbidding to marry, and commanding to abstain from meats, which God hath created to be received with thanksgiving of them which believe and

"THE BISHOP MUST BE…"

know the truth." Any teaching that contradicts the revealed will of God is "a doctrine of demons" and those who teach such doctrines have been seduced by deceiving spirits and must be rejected according to Galatians 1:8,9. We can also conclude that polygamy was forbidden. The practice of multiple wives and or mistresses was prohibited. For this is clearly established by the statement "husbands of one wife." Now is this gender specific because it says the "husband" of one wife, and not the spouse of one spouse? Well, the question that naturally arises as to whether a woman is qualified to hold the office of a bishop or any other office will not be addressed here, for it

"THE BISHOP MUST BE…"

can be an exhaustive subject with supporters on both sides of the argument. Instead let us focus at this time upon the principle of "hermeneutics" and only look at what the scripture is saying about "a bishop" not on whether it is exclusive to males.

Paul says the bishop must be…the husband of one wife. Where, is he drawing his conclusion from? What has shaped these suppositions? We are fortunate enough that he was wise enough to leave us a written account of his spiritual wisdom, revelation knowledge, and understanding. Consider Paul's letter to the Ephesians Church. He begins the 5th chapter by saying, "Therefore be imitators of Christ as dear children. And

"THE BISHOP MUST BE..."

walk in love…but fornicators and all uncleanliness or covertness, let it not even be named among you, as is fitting for saints…" Then in verse 21-32 we have his thesis upon marriage. In verse one he admonishes us to imitate Christ, how are we to imitate Christ in marriage? Well, he writes that Christ loves the Church and, laid down His life for it, then we as imitators ought to love and care as husbands and wives in the same manner. It is evident that there was only one sacrifice by Christ and that was for His bride. He shows fidelity by His actions towards His bride the Church. Therefore, husbands in particular ought to do the same whether they're bishops or not, because this is a foundational and

"THE BISHOP MUST BE…"

fundamental truth. We can see that Paul derives his doctrine from God's original intention for marriage. Paul in Romans 7 talks about the law of marriage. He concludes as long as a spouse is alive you are legally bound to that spouse, even if you have married another. He goes on to say that your second marriage does not become legal until the first spouse is deceased, and then and only then are you recognized in the eyes of God's perfect law (Psalms 19:7), as married to a second spouse. We must remember God designed man and woman to become one flesh, when they become married, only to be dissolved by death. He declared in Genesis 2:24 that "… a man leaves his father and his

"THE BISHOP MUST BE…"

mother, and shall cleave unto his wife: and they shall be one flesh." This signified a change in priority between husband and wife, towards one another. God's original intent was and still is one husband and one wife until death separates you. His design is always being altered by demon possessed individuals who have been deceived into thinking like Eve, that perhaps God isn't all-wise, all-knowing, or all-powerful, and we His created beings may know more than Him. That was Eve's seduction, don't let it be yours!

Jesus reiterated according to Mark's gospel what was said in Genesis. In Mark 10:7, Mark uses the Greek word "Proskollao" to

"THE BISHOP MUST BE…"

describe what Jesus meant, when He described the union between a husband and a wife. The word "Proshollao" means to glue to or cement together. This is an intensification of the marriage relationship of faithfulness, loyalty and permanence. Paul's thoughts on restricting a bishop to one wife becomes clearer, he knew that the culture at that time and throughout history would always be totally contradictive, to the concept of one spouse for life. He wanted the Church and especially its leaders to avoid the prevalent behavior in society of divorcing your spouses and marrying another for any ungodly reason.

"THE BISHOP MUST BE…"

In Paul's day people were marrying and remarrying because societies laws gave them license to do so. Paul knew that God's people and especially its leaders had to be a cut above reproach, and offer the world a better solution to their sin sick souls. He also surmised that knowing the true intent of marriage and seeing it displayed and all that is required in a marriage relationship it would be impossible for a person to be committed totally to several wives and still bc able to service the Church of the Living God.

Jesus said: "It hath been said, Whosoever shall put away his wife, let him give her a writing of divorcement: But I say unto you, That whosoever shall put away his wife,

"THE BISHOP MUST BE…"

saving for the cause of fornication, causeth her to commit adultery: and whosoever shall marry her that is divorced committeth adultery." (Matthew 5:31-32). The reason why God abhors divorce is because it was dissolution of what God had joined (Proskollao) together. Divorce by definition means to separate or disunite things closely connected; to force asunder. Divorce is a diverting, to divert means to turn off from any course, direction or intended purpose. To subvert, it is a disruption, a destabilizing, an overthrow, an undermining, a sabotaging of God's design for marriage.

Therefore, according to the law of marriage and divorce, a bishop was restricted from

"THE BISHOP MUST BE…"

multiple marriages if a spouse is alive, even though the law of the land said he was free to remarry. According to Jesus' teaching on the subject of divorce, it was only permitted by Moses "because of the hardness of your heart…" meaning that they would not be persuaded to keep their sworn vow to their chosen mate, and to avoid civil disorder, this civil rule was (not a spiritual principle) instituted. In this instance they extolled their will above God's will. But here Paul lays the foundation for leaders to be pristine examples of the will of God, one wife for life, a cementing of two lives together, as one, walking together as the Lord intended from the beginning. And if the leaders today

"THE BISHOP MUST BE..."

would be the pristine examples, then the world would follow. This requirement shows the world that the Church of Christ was and is different and that it had high standards and was beyond scrutiny. To peek into the culture at the time this was written tells us that putting away one's wife was common practice among the heathens, and quite possibly many within the Church. And if anyone wanted this great office of the bishop his past and present marriage relationship had to be blameless. Here we see the first requirement to be blameless effects every other requirement.

"THE BISHOP MUST BE…"

As the culture around the early Church permitted divorce and or multiple spouses, the bishop was required to be above this sort of behavior and be committed to the outstanding life changing principles of God. Part of his qualification was and still is to be the husband of one wife, no deviations, no variations, from the principles of God, "a person against whom no evil can be proved; one who is everywhere invulnerable."

"THE BISHOP MUST BE…"

4

Vigilant

Paul the Apostle continues his revelation to Timothy concerning the office of the bishop, he invokes the word "vigilant." Some bible translations, translate the word vigilant as temperate. To be temperate means to be moderate; not excessive. Moderate in the indulgence of the appetites and passions. Cool; calm; not marked with passion; not violent; as a temperate discourse or address; temperate language. Paul uses the Greek word "nephaleos" (nay-Fal'-ee-os), it suggests that the bishop must be sober which is not a reference to wine, but goes much

"THE BISHOP MUST BE…"

deeper than that, because, the very next verse Paul addresses the necessity of not being addicted to wine. Here vigilant (sober) means serious, sensible, and solemn. It means having a sober view, it means to be circumspect, which conveys the thought derived from the Latin words circumspectus, and circumspicere- which means to "look around," this is originated from "circum" 'around about' + "specere" 'look.' Which, intimates that a bishop being vigilant is to keep careful watch for possible danger or difficulties. He is the watchman of the flock and must 'keep awake." He must be vigil, alert, careful, cautious, circumspect,

"THE BISHOP MUST BE…"

watchful. He as the bishop or overseer must always be on the lookout.

Look at what Paul tells Timothy in the fourth chapter of first Timothy. He speaks about the assault upon the Church and sound doctrine. Therefore, anyone that desires this office must be aware that they will have to have definitive character traits that hopefully are innate or highly developed before one ascertains the office of the bishop. Vigilance is an essential attribute that a bishop must have, or all the other qualities will become negatively influenced, because of the lack of vigilance. The New King James Version uses the word "temperate" which proposes a meaning of showing moderation or self-

"THE BISHOP MUST BE…"

restraint. I would concur that a bishop must exhibit these virtuous qualities, but vigilance I believe most closely conveys the message that apostle Paul wanted to instill in Timothy and any individual that had a desire to lead in the Church of the Living God. I want to reiterate that the apostle Paul expressly wanted Timothy and overseers to be sober in the sense that they were to be serious, sensible, and solemn. Serious in the sense that they were to be candidates that are thoughtful in character and manner; acting and speaking earnestly. Sensible in course of action, and in statements in accordance with wisdom, and prudence, beneficial for all people. If the bishop be prudent, then he will

"THE BISHOP MUST BE…"

be demonstrating care and thought for the present as well as for the future of those he leads. He also must be solemn, which is to say he is composed, serious in conduct, and this qualifies him to be worthy of respect.

William Burkitt's Expository Notes, expresses the opinion that being vigilant a bishop is: "very diligent and watchful in the performance of his whole duty, not long absent from his flock, nor negligent when he is among them."

Jamieson-Fausett-Brown Commentary, on the vigilance of the bishop states: "ever on the watch, as sober men alone can be; keenly alive, so as to foresee what ought to be done."

1 Thessalonians 5:6-8 Therefore let us not

"THE BISHOP MUST BE…"

sleep, as do others; but let us watch and be sober. For they that sleep, sleep in the night; and they that be drunken are drunken in the night. But let us, who are of the day, be sober, putting on the breastplate of faith and love; and for a helmet, the hope of salvation.

"THE BISHOP MUST BE…"

5

Sober

Now we come to understand what Paul describes as being "sober." He transcribes the Greek word "Sophron" (so'-Frone), which is defined as safe (sound) in mind, self-controlled. It's a compound word " sozo"- "safe" to save, deliver or protect an "phren"- to reign in or curb the feelings, the mind. When combining these two words it helps us to understand that a bishop must be sound in mind, able to control his passions except those passions for the Lord Jesus Christ, His glorious gospel and the care and nurture of the Church of God.

"THE BISHOP MUST BE…"

Sober is a condition that must be protected and nurtured at all times, because without it the entire office of the bishop as overseer is weakened, and subject to reproach, and unnecessary scrutiny. It must be interwoven into the character and life of the candidate, and should become contagious so that it is active in the lives of the flock of God. Why? For it is a nurturing attribute where the one who exhibits it is always concerned about the welfare of people and their relationship to Christ, and if they're lacking or straying, he considers what he can do to bring them back into a greater relationship with the God of all salvation. He is not only able to reign in his

"THE BISHOP MUST BE…"

emotion or feelings, but he truly demonstrates the ability to reach those who are in ominous need of deliverance and can easily employ his ability to guide them in. The bishop isn't an individual who flies off the handle when things aren't going as desired, but he has the self-control to remain consistent in Christ-likeness, and be temperate until the situation is resolved. The bishop's mind must be "set," "firm" and "steadfast" in the knowledge of Jesus Christ, and determined not to be shaken by anything. He must be "Sophron" sober.

The International Standard Encyclopedia expressed the following thought with regards to being sober.

"THE BISHOP MUST BE…"

The verbs sophroneo and sophronizo; adverb sophronos, "of sound mind," and sophronizo; "self-possessed," "without excesses of any kind," "moderate and discreet." In Mk 5:15; Lu 8:35, "sane," said of one out of whom demons had just been cast. In the Pastoral Epistles, this virtue is especially commended to certain classes, because of extravagances characterizing particular periods of life, that had to be guarded against, namely, to aged men, with reference to the querulousness of old age (Titus 2:2); to young men, with reference to their sanguine views of life, and their tendency to disregard consequences (Titus 2:6); enjoined upon young women, with reference to extravagance in dress and

"THE BISHOP MUST BE…"

speech (Titus 2:5; 1Tim. 2:9); and, in a similar manner, commended to ministers, because of the importance of their judgment and conduct, as teachers and exemplars (1Tim. 3:2).

Here it is clear that all leaders and all believers are required, be sober, clear thinking, which the scriptures clearly command. "A bishop then must be blameless, the husband of one wife, vigilant, sober…" Soberness has the added connotation of "watchfulness" (De 4:9; Ps 39:1; Mt 26:41; Ac 20:31; 1Co 10:12; 16:13; Col 4:2; 1Pe 5:8; Re 3:2), and diligently keeping of oneself (De 4:9; 23:9; Ac 15:29; 1Ti 5:22; Jas 1:27; 1Jo 5:21; Jude 1:21).

"THE BISHOP MUST BE…"

Perhaps the word prudent would come nearer to the meaning of the apostle than any single word which we have. Scripture portrays the prudent as being wise "The wisdom of the prudent is to understand his way: but the folly of fools is deceit. (Proverbs 14:8)." "The prudent man looketh well to his going (Proverbs 14:15)." The sober or prudent person therefore, is cautious; circumspect; one who is practically wise; very careful of the consequences of enterprises, measures or actions; and extremely cautious not to act when the end is of doubtful benefit, or probably impracticable. Again, the bible states in Proverbs 22:3 "A prudent man foreseeth the evil and hideth himself."

"THE BISHOP MUST BE…"

A prudent man, by the help of his prudence will have foresight because he is sober-minded and not inebriated will forsake the way that is contrary to the will of God and will be guided by the Holy Spirit to bring forth the true plan of God that pertains to the Church of God. The highest wisdom of men is to hide

themselves in this sanctuary; to neglect it is their recklessness and ruin.

1 Thessalonians 5:5-6 Ye are all the children of light, and the children of the day: we are not of the night, nor of darkness. Therefore, let us not sleep, as do others; but let us watch and be sober.

"THE BISHOP MUST BE…"

6

Of Good Behavior...

Good behavior? What is that all about? Why is it necessary to state that aspirants must exude "good behavior?"

Psalm 25:21 speaks of honesty and integrity. Integrity meaning a person has the qualities of being honest and having strong moral principles. It also implies that one's state of mind is that of being whole and undivided. From the text we understand that good behavior means that one must be "decorous." That is in keeping with good taste and propriety; polite and restrained. It may also be defined as proper, seemly, decent,

"THE BISHOP MUST BE…"

becoming, befitting, tasteful, tactful, suitable, fitting, fit; polite, well mannered, well behaved, genteel, refined, polished, well bred, dignified, respectable, courtly, civilized; formal, reserved, modest, demure, sedate, staid. There is no room for anything other than the occupants of the office to be. The absence of a historical pattern of behavior will most assuredly disqualify any and all candidates from the office of the bishop. The one who assumes the office must first pass the test to be qualified, he cannot have a history of mishandling or neglecting life's responsibilities through habitual poor decision making, whether it's through error or deliberately and expect to assume such an

"THE BISHOP MUST BE…"

important position in the church of the Living God. Good behavior is an asset not a convenient luxury you can turn on at moment's notice. It must be embedded within the individual upon examination for the office, not something to acquire after. We must remember that these qualities are required so that the church of God can flourish without reproach.

Three things happen when the unqualified are consecrated into this and any office unworthily. First the name of Christ is not hallowed in the hearts and mind of believers and nonbelievers. As it is written "For the name of God is blasphemed among the

"THE BISHOP MUST BE…"

Gentiles through you…" (Romans 2:24). Second the local assembly becomes a damaged testimony for God because if the head isn't right, the rest of the body falters and becomes out of sync with the Holy Spirit and becomes a Laodicean ministry. Third the leader himself begins to miss the move of the Spirit of God and eventually relies unwittingly upon the flesh to accomplish the vision. Never realizing that anything that is tainted by flesh cannot please God and is absolutely unacceptable by Him.

One of Timothy's most pressing duties was to take care that those who held office in the churches were beyond reproach. Therefore,

"THE BISHOP MUST BE…"

the tone of the Christian community is largely that of its leaders, so he must be beyond reproach. The effect of a good minister will be spoiled if a man yields to foolish levity or intemperate habits. Moderation, serenity of temper, are signs that an individual may aspire to the sacred work of the ministry; and these are the very qualities which we should look for in candidates for every office in the body of Christ, more than those of rhetoric, brilliance, or outward attractiveness.

A person Given to Hospitality…

This meant he was to exude this quality, and that people knew him to be such a person. If we were to define the word hospitality we could find more than a few synonyms, such

"THE BISHOP MUST BE…"

as: warm-heartedness, kindness, kindheartedness, congeniality, geniality, sociability. This meant the person of the bishop had to be, a person having a kind and sympathetic nature. To say they were congenial was to say they were, a pleasant person because of a personality, and qualities. They were also sociable and affable, meaning that they were friendly and good natured.

Apt to Teach…

The last part of 1 Timothy 3:2 stated by Paul the Apostle declares, that a bishop must be apt, (able (NKJV) to teach. As defined by Webster's New College Dictionary, the word "apt" means: suited to its purpose. Which

"THE BISHOP MUST BE…"

conveys the thought that if one desired the office of a bishop he must be able to communicate Christian teaching, he must be skilled in the conveyance of sound Christian doctrine (Galatians 1:6-9).

In other words, he must be fit or have the ability to teach before he can be considered for the office of a bishop, this is why a novice or immature Christians are exempt from the position, although one may have a desire, he would be deemed unfit for entrance into the bishopric, until they exuded qualities of mature Christian characteristics that are in absolute agreement with that which makes one a qualified candidate for the maintenance of the office of a bishop.

"THE BISHOP MUST BE…"

The Believer's Bible commentary, expresses it in this manner, "An elder must be able to teach as he visits those with spiritual problems; he must be able to turn to the scriptures and explain the will of God in such matters. He must be able to feed the flock of God (1 Peter 5:2) and to use the scripture in refuting those who bring false doctrines (Acts 20:29-31). It does not necessarily mean that a bishop must have the gift of teaching, but rather that in his house-to-house ministries as well as in the assembly, he can set forth the doctrines of faith and rightly divide the Word of Truth, and is ready

"THE BISHOP MUST BE…"

and keen to do it" (Believer's Bible Commentary p.2087, William MacDonald).

Apostle Paul reiterates his message regarding the qualifications of a bishop in his epistle to Titus, he writes: "For a bishop must be…" And in verse 9 admonishes Titus that a bishop must be…without ambiguity, "Holding fast the faithful word as he hath been taught, that he may be able by sound doctrine both to exhort and to convince the gainsayers (Titus 1:7,9)."

Here as in his epistle to Timothy, the message is the same, that a bishop must be sound in doctrine, meaning he is to be uncorrupted and

"THE BISHOP MUST BE…"

true in doctrine, with no hint of ambivalence. The calling requires the leadership to be grounded in the faithful word of God, and expressly promulgate it.

Not given to wine…

And the LORD spake unto Aaron, saying, Do not drink wine nor strong drink, thou, nor thy sons with thee, when ye go into the tabernacle of the congregation, lest ye die: it shall be a statute forever throughout your generations: And that ye may put difference between holy and unholy, and between unclean and clean; And that ye may teach the children of Israel all the statutes which the

"THE BISHOP MUST BE…"

LORD hath spoken unto them by the hand of Moses. (Lev. 10:8-11 KJV).

Immediately after the rebellion of Aaron's sons Nadab and Abihu, God speaks to Aaron regarding the strict conduct of the priests. Prior to the Lord speaking to Aaron, Moses, tells Aaron what the Lord spoke. He says "This is what the Lord spoke, 'By those who come to Me I must be regarded as holy; And before all the people I must be glorified.'" (Lev. 10:3 NKJV). Establishing the fact that leadership must maintain an exemplary behavior at all times and nothing must be allowed to intrude upon their service unto the Lord. Leadership must always be consciously aware of any and all pitfalls that may arise to

"THE BISHOP MUST BE…"

deter them from their sacred mission, and whatever may inhibit them they must steer clear from. Therefore, Aaron the high priest conveys this prohibition of the Lord. "Do not drink wine nor strong drink…" Here the command not to drink wine or intoxicating drink was given because it would impair their ability to make wise decisions. There could be nothing that has the possibility to convolute the mind impairing the judgment to decipher between holy and unholy. The mind of a leader must always be sharpened by the influence of the Holy Spirit not be made a prisoner to the profane. The Bishop must be…the administer of holy things and to do

"THE BISHOP MUST BE…"

that he must not only be of a sober mind but also guard against those outward

influences that would seek to rob him of his duty to be holy as God is Holy. The bishop, as, the priest is because of the very nature of their assignments are required to be what God would be amongst the people, since their example is supposed to typify the lifestyle that God wants all His people to exemplify, there could be absolutely no deviation whatsoever.

"Not give to wine" is a precaution that speaks to the influence of other spirits' influence over us as believers, which must be avoided at all costs. This type of spirit usually brings

"THE BISHOP MUST BE…"

about all the wrong decisions when persons are under its influence. The true admonition is to avoid alcohol; we have all seen its

detrimental effects, and as a leader it can hinder and disrupt the move of God!

"No Striker…"

A better translation of this word would be, not to be violent. Today when we hear the word striker, it draws us into thinking of an employee on strike. But here the word has very serious implications for the person who would ascend to the office of a bishop.

For a bishop must have self-control if he's going to oversee the church of God. He

"THE BISHOP MUST BE…"

cannot be prone to fits of violence. Just imagine if you were in a relationship with someone whose behavior involved physical force. One moment they are as gentle as a lamb, and in a fraction of a second later they've lost all composure and transformed into someone unrecognizable, with malicious intent in their heart. This would seem to be a person that isn't in control of their temperament. It is not a problem of getting angry, because in the course of life there will always be things that goes against the grain. The problem is when we get angry does it cause us to sin in thought, words, or actions. If it isn't brought under control, it will lead one to become as Cain, where we would be,

"THE BISHOP MUST BE…"

guilty, of slaying our brother in Christ, or a potential brother or sister in Christ.

In his letter to his son in the gospel, Paul expressed the exact sentiment to a young pastor named Titus in Crete. He said to Titus "For a bishop must be blameless, as the steward of God; not self-willed, not soon angry, not given to wine, no striker…" This gives us an absolutely clear understanding of the message to be conveyed to the potential adherer to the position of a bishop.

"Not Greedy for Filthy Lucre… (a.k.a. Money)"
This brings to mind the question, that always needs to be asked and answered. The

"THE BISHOP MUST BE…"

question is: what are you in it for? Is it to gain wealth as some have used the position to gain immense wealth. Is it to serve God and bring Him glory and honor? Is it to lead souls from an eternal hell into the marvelous light of Jesus Christ?

The last two answers should be the only reasons for entrance into this holy position of overseer also known as the bishopric. Any other reason makes you a charlatan, and a prostitute of the gospel which makes it and you a deliverer of a false gospel, and according to Galatians 1-8-10; "But though we, or an angel from heaven, preach any other gospel unto you than that which we have preached unto you, let him be accursed.

"THE BISHOP MUST BE…"

As we said before, so say I now again, If any man preaches any other gospel unto you than that ye have received, let him be accursed. For do I now persuade men, or God? or do I seek to please men? for if I yet pleased men, I should not be the servant of Christ."

This sums up our motives if it is not in the sincere service of Christ then whatever we are doing is for our own pleasure in the service of our flesh not the Spirit.

I will say so-called ministers of the gospel of Christ have become very lucrative preaching and teaching the gospel, a lot of times to the detriment of their followers. I say their

"THE BISHOP MUST BE…"

followers because if they were to allow themselves to be true followers of Christ Jesus then the church of the Living God would be leading the world into righteousness, not the world dictating to the culture what is right and wrong. We have an obscured view of the reality of the Gospel of Jesus Christ when we believe that the raising of fund$ is more important than the altar call. When a minster asks you to give an offering and never digs into his or her own pocket to pull out whatever they are asking you for. Beware of the sideshow hustle!

"THE BISHOP MUST BE…"

Again, Paul instructs Titus of the same thing, if love of money is your motivating factor, this position is not for you!!!

"But Patient…"

The New King James Version of the Bible says: "but gentle…" Both words derive their meaning from the Greek, epieikes; Strong's #1933: From "epi," "Unto," and "eikos," "likely." The word suggests a character that is equitable, responsible, forbearing, moderate, fair, and considerate. It is the opposite of harsh, abrasive, sarcastic, cruel, and contentious. The person with epieikes does not insist on the letter of the law.

"THE BISHOP MUST BE…"

So, the bishop must in addition to all the other qualifying characteristics must also exude patience. If not, he is definitely unqualified to assume the position of a bishop. Isn't it interesting to note that if a candidate for bishop comes up short in one of these qualifications he isn't fit for the office. As a candidate you must have a certain maturity level where you are no longer ruled by impatience, but by the spirit of the Living God. Nothing qualifies you more than to be ruled not by the flesh, but, by the Spirit of the Living God. That is what this is all about your spiritual maturity. You would have been tested in these areas and only when you have

"THE BISHOP MUST BE…"

come through consistently with flying colors are you able to be considered for the bishopric. "But let patience have her perfect work, that ye may be perfect and entire, wanting nothing." (James 1:4).

"THE BISHOP MUST BE…"

7

"Not a Brawler"

A brawler conveys the idea of someone that is quarrelsome. It is someone that is augmentative, disputatious, contentious, confrontational. A brawler is a moody person, who may also be an unreasonable individual, whom people may always want to avoid. This is the type of person whom you can't receive or receive from because you see them as disingenuous.

It would be a disadvantage for the church of God to employ any such person, especially an individual in any kind of a leadership role.

"THE BISHOP MUST BE…"

All Christian believers are to measure up to a high standard of Christ likeness, and to be insincere, untruthful, deceitful, misleading and hypocritical tarnishes the office and is an insult to Christ who was the total opposite of a brawler.

The American Standard Version of the bible conveys the message to the bishop this way. "no brawler, no striker; but gentle, not contentious…" (1 Tim. 3:3 ASV). Here we understand that to be a brawler meant that you had the temperament to be violent and or contentious in behavior, instead of the Christlike fruit of the Spirit attribute of gentleness

"THE BISHOP MUST BE…"

(Gal. 5:22). If you had a reputation in the past of a short-tempered volatile person and have not put that in the hands of the Holy Spirit to change you, then how can you expect to change others? My spiritual forefathers use to say; "that flesh is a mess!" James sums it up in his epistle in the following way. "From whence *come* wars and fightings among you? *come they* not hence, *even* of your lusts that war in your members?" (James 4:1). Again, the American Standard Version sums it this way, "…come they not hence, even of your pleasures that war in your members? (James 4:1). He talks about where the issue originates from. The problem stems from your lustfulness and the desire to satisfy

"THE BISHOP MUST BE…"

yourselves. It is the inner workings that must first be delt with prior to consideration of the office of the bishop. If we or a potential bishop has not mortified the deeds of the body it disqualifies us all from serving Christ in any capacity. For what would the fruit if that labor be? We must never forget that anything the flesh produces cannot please God, because the flesh is and always will be enmity towards God.

The mentality and understanding that is needed today among us as believers is that if we died with Christ, we must also believe that we shall also live with him. And our lifestyle

"THE BISHOP MUST BE…"

should at all times emulate the fact that we are Christ-like, not the fleshly-type.

The bishop therefore cannot be swayed by what he'd (his flesh) like to do but what would Jesus do. The bishop has a tremendous responsibility to care for the people of God to prepare them for kingdom work and to be ever ready for the coming of the Lord Jesus Christ. To achieve this mission, he too must be prepared because he will definitely be put to the test over and over again. He can't afford to have the slightest crack in his armor of character to be exploited, but must put on the entire armor of Christ that he will be able to stand against all the wiles of the enemy.

"THE BISHOP MUST BE..."

8

"Not Covetous"

But fornication, and all uncleanness, or covetousness, let it not be once named among you, as becometh saints;

Neither filthiness, nor foolish talking, nor jesting, which are not convenient: but rather giving of thanks.

For this ye know, that no whoremonger, nor unclean person, nor covetous man, who is an idolater, hath any inheritance in the kingdom of Christ and of God. (Ephesians 5:3-5)

The instructions are clear for the individual or individuals who would seek to occupy this

"THE BISHOP MUST BE…"

office as an overseer of the Church of Jesus Christ. There was absolutely no room for the lusts of the flesh, the lust of the eye, or the pride of life. His mind needed to be in tact so that he would not fall prey to those very things that use to ensnare him. Just like every other believer, the bishop needed to keep himself from all filthiness that would put a stain on his life. The bishop had to exceed a lifestyle that was above and beyond impeachment. Paul reiterates the fact that a bishop could not, under any circumstances be covetous.

The question here isn't why, but why not? The reason being is that a covetous person is

"THE BISHOP MUST BE…"

an individual eager for gain, if he is avaricious, it means he is a defrauder, and his motives are most likely motivated by greediness. Here in Ephesians 5:3 the word covetous stems from *pleton* which means "more," and *echo* which means "to have." Together they express the state of having more, and this will to have more leads a person to defraud others. Jesus gave several warnings of the inherit dangers of covetousness. Mark conveyed Jesus' words *"Thefts, covetousness, wickedness, deceit, lasciviousness, an evil eye, blasphemy, pride, foolishness: All these evil things come from within, and defile the man. (Mark 7:22-23).*

"THE BISHOP MUST BE..."

Luke also expresses Christ's thoughts regarding covetousness, "And he said unto them, Take heed, and beware of covetousness: for a man's life consisteth not in the abundance of the things which he possesseth." *(Luke 12:15).* The apostle Paul in his summation of the downward spiral of mankind unto more and more degradation, he says: "Being filled with all unrighteousness, fornication, wickedness, covetousness, maliciousness; full of envy, murder, debate, deceit, malignity; whisperers, Backbiters, haters of God, despiteful, proud, boasters, inventors of evil things, disobedient to parents, Without understanding, covenant breakers, without natural affection,

"THE BISHOP MUST BE…"

implacable, unmerciful: Who knowing the judgment of God, that they which commit such things are worthy of death, not only do the same, but have pleasure in them that do them." *(Romans 1:29-32).*

He also expresses the same feeling regarding covetousness when addressing the Church at Colossae; "Mortify therefore your members which are upon the earth; fornication, uncleanness, inordinate affection, evil concupiscence, and covetousness, which is idolatry…" (Colossians 3:5).

So, the answer to the question, Why not? Is because, covetousness is idolatry. It is nothing more than the desire for filthy lucre

"THE BISHOP MUST BE…"

over the leading and advancement of God's ecclesia. Idolatry always puts the needs of self before the purpose and plans of the Living God. And as a bishop your primary functions are service to God Almighty and the people of God whom you have been ordained and consecrated to serve.

Remember the office of a bishop is an office of service to the people of God, not a place to set up your throne to rule over the people like the Nicolaitans. But it is an office where you must meet the needs of the office. Nowhere did the apostle say that the office of a bishop is for you to receive accolades, and sit in the finest seats, or be escorted in and out of the sanctuary having little or no contact with the

"THE BISHOP MUST BE…"

people of God. No! Mr. and Madam bishop your chief functions have been distorted over time and seduced you into to believing that you're the one to be served and you should be the center of attention, and that the show doesn't start without you and all things have to meet your strictest expectations. This is why not!? Because idolatry is a subtle spirit and if you're not careful even those with the best intention, must be… careful of covetousness, because the bishop cannot be, he must be…untarnished by this deadly infectious spirit of covetousness.

"THE BISHOP MUST BE..."

9

"One that rules his house well"

"One that ruleth well his own house, having his children in subjection with all gravity..."

One that rules his house well, is an essential and mostly overlooked requirement for all occupants for this highly sought after position of our day. What we need to understand first and foremost is this command was given to keep unqualified and unfit individuals from influencing and directing the lives of the Church of Jesus Christ.

Ruling expresses continuous or repeated action. It is a quality that demanded that the

"THE BISHOP MUST BE…"

potential office holder must *"be"* and continuously *"be."* There wasn't any room for him to be anything else but a person of consistent and express character to maintain and unchangeable demeanor. The demand for such a trait was not a foreign entity but was already ingrained in the purpose of God. The patriarch Abraham was one standard bearer. God speaks of him and his character as a man who rules his household very well.

"For I know him, that he will command his children and his household after him, and they shall keep the way of the LORD, to do justice and judgment; that the LORD may bring upon Abraham that which he hath spoken of him." (Genesis 18:19).

God was well aware of Abraham being a man of faith and character and his determination

"THE BISHOP MUST BE…"

to always be a man of outstanding character which certified him to rule. This is a model for all adherents who seek this sanctified office of the bishop. He must be, not become. Before he desires such a lofty aspiration he must ***already be!*** Joshua testifies his position for service when he proclaimed; *"but as for me and my house, we will serve the LORD."*

The Psalmist reiterates Joshua's sentiments when he states: "I will behave myself wisely in a perfect way…I will walk within my house with a perfect heart. I will set no wicked thing before mine eyes…it shall not cleave to me. A froward heart shall depart from me…He that worketh deceit shall not dwell within my house: he that telleth lies shall not tarry in my sight." (Psalms 101: 2-4, 7).

The centurion of Acts 10 had an outside testimony of being a devout man, that feared God with all his house. His life style of prayer and alms giving had come before God as a

"THE BISHOP MUST BE…"

memorial. He is exemplary of and individual who God saw as an honorable man maintaining the attributes of management that our Lord identifies as admirable.

"If any be blameless, the husband of one wife, having faithful children not accused of riot or unruly." (Titus 1:6). These are the ones who may be considered for the office of a bishop. Anything less than the highest standards is an abuse of the office and brings about shame on the individual and possible irreparable damage to the body of Christ.

The apostle Paul sums up the characteristic of the bishop that rules his house well in a godly manner not as a tyrant, when he writes to his son in the gospel Titus; *"In all things shewing thyself a pattern of good works: in doctrine shewing uncorruptness, gravity, sincerity,"* (Titus 2:7).

Paul is admonishing the urgency of us all, but especially the potential and or current office holders, ***to be*** and not to fall into the trap of Eli the high priest who vacated his responsibility of maintaining the sanctity of the Tabernacle, of his office and his home and suffered the loss of his children and the loss of his anointing. *"For I have told him that I*

"THE BISHOP MUST BE..."

will judge his house for ever for the iniquity which he knoweth; because his sons made themselves vile, and he restrained them not." (1 Samuel 3:13).

"THE BISHOP MUST BE…"

10

"Not a Novice…"

A novice is a beginner, learner, trainee, apprentice, greenhorn, neophyte, rookie. A novice is a person who is entering a profession without prior experience.

1 Timothy 3:6 *"An elder must not be a new believer, because he might become proud, and the devil would cause him to fall.*
(NLT Life Application Study Bible, Second Edition (Function). Kindle Edition.)

An elder is not a new convert nor is he unlearned, untrained in the oracles of the Living God. Anyone who comes into a particular occupation must be educated in the aspects of the specific job requirements. As

"THE BISHOP MUST BE…"

he progresses, he develops the necessary skills for advancement. He would testify that when he first began, he didn't realize all of the intricacies of the requirements of his position and he was unprepared to assume a higher position. Life teaches us that we progress from infancy, to toddler, to child, to adolescence and then young adulthood before we can begin to surmise any of the complexities of adulthood. You give milk to a baby, but at some point, that baby must begin to grow and be feed by something more than milk. He must grow to eat solid food or he will eventually become malnourished. No one shall seek the office of bishop that is spiritually and scripturally, malnourished.

"THE BISHOP MUST BE…"

This person **will** corrupt the office through their immaturity.

If a young believer is selected to the bishopric the same spirit that brought Lucifer's downfall will bring about their demise. Pride and arrogance *("Pride goeth before destruction, and a haughty spirit before a fall." (Proverbs 16:18)* was the devils downfall. Therefore, young believers must become stable and spiritually sound in the faith before contemplation of a rise to any leadership role in the church. This is done often in the church because of the desperation for workers before their faith has reached maturity. All believers should have

"THE BISHOP MUST BE…"

responsibility in service, but not before they are firmly grounded in their faith with a solidly observable Christ-like lifestyle and an exemplary knowledge of the Word of God!

"THE BISHOP MUST BE…"

11

"Moreover, he must have a good report…"

This is a truthful saying, if a man desires the office of a bishop and all the responsibilities and privileges that are innate with the office, he is desiring a good thing. Therefore, a bishop **must** have a good testimony **"…of them which are without."** The idea expressed here is that the person who desires to assume the bishopric, must be an undisputable example to those outside the church walls. His character must be able to withstand outside scrutiny There should never be any who can bring an assault upon the bishop's office to impeach the character

"THE BISHOP MUST BE…"

and or qualifications to occupy the bishop's office. If there ever arises a character flaw then the candidate is unfit to hold office, even though he may meet every other prerequisite. The standard is all not one, not some but every one of them. His position demands a strict adherence to the criterion put forth in scripture.

Since scripture is infallible then the requirements listed within them are infallibly unfailing and irrevocable. How a bishop carries out their duties as citizens, neighbors, family and friends facilitates or infuriates the ability to communicate the gospel of Christ.

"THE BISHOP MUST BE…"

Does the behavior of the potential candidate help or hinder the church of Christ to carry out its mission in society? The bishop must be a bridge builder amongst unbelievers in order to spread the gospel to non-believers.

The Greek word **maturia,** *(mar-too-ree'-ah)* is defined as evidence given. It is derived from the noun **matureo,** and means to witness…the opposite of *maturia,* is **pseudomaturia,** which means a false witness, which would make any potential candidate unworthy for occupation of the office of the bishop. The potential candidate and its resident occupants must be emphatically

"THE BISHOP MUST BE…"

worthy to serve the Church of God because Jesus fulfilled all the requirements to be the savior of the world, therefore a bishop must be able to uphold the standard required for his calling. This way he avoids all the pitfalls that the devil will send his way. Preparation starts before anyone thinks of attaining the office of the bishop. Trying to meet the standards after is a recipe for disaster.

"THE BISHOP MUST BE..."

12

The Bishop Today

Bishop's today, are much different from the first century bishop. Today we have bishops from various denominations, all with the claim of direct descendance from the first century church.

Today it would seem that there is a stark difference in appearance and functionality than when Paul was writing to his son in the gospel Timothy regarding the specific qualifications for office. Twenty-first century bishops appear to have assumed a more monarchal status and position in the world and the church. Some may say that the church

"THE BISHOP MUST BE..."

must serve the bishop instead of the bishop being consecrated to serve his or her local congregations, and to neglect such fealty to a bishop is to reject the ordained order of God Himself. Some rule with absolute authority, neglecting the established order of the church where elders are to be a vibrant aspect of church authority. Yet some denominations pride themselves on episcopal order and the sole rule of the episcopacy.

The Apostle Paul never instructed the church to implement and maintain a hierarchy within the church. Twice in the book of Revelation Christ's messages to the seven churches, the

"THE BISHOP MUST BE…"

Nicolaitanes are mentioned (2:6; 3:15). The first mention was a commendation of them for not allowing their particular infiltrations inside the church. The second was a rebuke to the church at Pergamos for allowing the Nicolaitanes doctrine to subvert the church and become the standard. The Nicolaitanes were by definition:

(The nikolaitōn - from nikaō, to conquer, and laos, people. The business of those who wish to abuse their position to control people.) (du Toit, Francois. Mirror Study Bible (p. 2563). (Function). Kindle Edition.)

This practice God hates. He very much dislikes the monarchial absolute authoritarian rule of His church.

Most bishops today have a defined role as to what their service should be, most of the time

"THE BISHOP MUST BE…"

it's an absolute neglect of sola-scriptura. Scripture alone is the one and only determining factor of the function and authority of the office holder. When Paul wrote to Timothy and Titus regarding the functions of the overseer/elder he granted no absolute authority. He submitted the service of the bishop, without fanfare. He pointed out that it was "work." If there is a desire he says, then, "he desireth a good **work.**" No where is it found that believers must bow and kiss the ring. Jesus took a towel and washed His disciples' feet. How many bishops have you seen that would bend down and wash the feet of their congregants?

"THE BISHOP MUST BE…"

The bishopric is a servant of the local congregation and any assemblies they may minister to. We forget that a minister is first a servant of Christ and has been given a duty to shepherd Christ's church. A minister is an attendant, his job is to care for, comfort, support, look after, and aid the church of the Living God. Not to sit in a chair of adornment as the revered most holy person. He or she is not nor will they ever be the vicar of Christ.

I have had on several occasions been privy to work alongside a few bishops some who served the office admirably, and some with questionable intent.

"THE BISHOP MUST BE…"

The late great bishop James F. Copeland was one of those men whose service to the local as well as to the entire body of Christ is an example of the genuine exercising of the functions and qualifications of the office holder. He received many of accolades from those

within and without as to the love of God and the desire to serve God's people and to help facilitate the redemption of mankind. Under his leadership he would assure the local assemblies' needs were taken care of because God had put their care upon him as an overseer. As a result, other ministries gravitated not to the person in the office but the anointing upon the officer holder. He was

"THE BISHOP MUST BE…"

anointed to serve and that was his only motivation. He loved outreach ministry and use it as a tool to win the lost to Christ through home and foreign missions. The hungry were feed, the naked were clothed, the needs of many were meet through ministry. This type of ministry was and is in violent contrast to others I have witnessed. I have seen the bishopric be used to advance individual ministries, through authoritarianism. Some have used gimmicks to persuade through deception to give monetarily to advance their cause, such as "a first fruit offering" using Old Testament terms to guilt the congregation into supporting their personal ministry. Also, they

"THE BISHOP MUST BE…"

use scripture to guilt people into giving through stories of people that have been blessed, never ever producing that person to testify to their truth. They stand before a congregation and declare the "holy spirit spoke to them and told them a certain amount of people here are destined to give a certain amount of money." Usually, it isn't $10 it could start as high as $5000 or as low $100, and sometimes they add a specific thing that God is going to do for the individual. And finally, they come back to the rest because every penny counts (so bring your measly $10).

"THE BISHOP MUST BE…"

This has never been the intent for the office of the bishop. Remember this is and always has been a volunteer position. No where do I see in scripture that you were called to be a bishop. On the contrary it is a position that one chose as a service to the body of Christ. Yes, it has its benefits, and yes there are privileges to the holder of the office but the utmost expectation is service to God and His ecclesia.

www.ingramcontent.com/pod-product-compliance
Lightning Source LLC
Chambersburg PA
CBHW071218160426
43196CB00012B/2338